TURNING POOP INTO POWER FUEL

Clara MacCarald

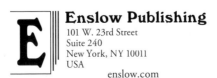
Enslow Publishing
101 W. 23rd Street
Suite 240
New York, NY 10011
USA

enslow.com

Words to Know

battery An object that uses chemicals to make electricity.

biocrude A fuel oil made from organic matter.

biogas A gas fuel made from rotting organic matter.

digesters Sealed bins set up to encourage fermentation.

digestion The process of breaking down food into things the body can use.

fermentation The process of tiny organisms such as bacteria and yeast breaking apart a substance.

greenhouse gases Substances that contribute to the warming of the earth's atmosphere.

hydrogen An element that is usually a gas and that burns easily.

methane A simple gas that burns easily.

wastewater treatment plant A place that treats water that has been used in homes or businesses.

Contents

A Load of Power

Wherever there are people, there is poop. Over seven billion people live on planet Earth, with over 323 million in the United States alone. That's a lot of waste! What do we do with it all? In most places, anything flushed down the toilet ends up in **wastewater treatment plants**.

We find poop gross for a very good reason: it's a health risk. If poop went into the water or land without being treated, it could make us all sick. Once it's been made safer, some ends up in trash dumps or on farm fields to grow crops. But some poop is also used for power fuel. Poop can produce electricity and make cars go. Someday, it might make spaceships fly!

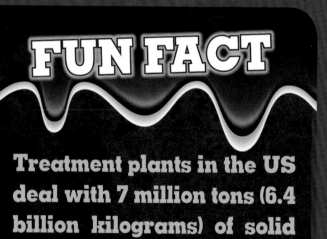

FUN FACT

Treatment plants in the US deal with 7 million tons (6.4 billion kilograms) of solid stuff every year!

Wastewater treatment plants slow down the flow of sewage in huge tanks to help the poop drop out.

We'll never make all the fuel we need using poop. But we can make a lot of it. And poop is a renewable source of power—it just keeps coming down the pipes!

What Is Poop, Anyway?

Everyone knows poop. They know it when they see it—and when they smell it. Yuck! But what exactly is it?

Poop is made of things our body doesn't need or can't use. Indigestible food ends up in poop. Stuff from our gut does, too. All people have a population of bacteria inside them, even if they're not sick. These good bacteria finish the process of **digestion** in the large intestine. Thanks, bacteria! As poop moves through our

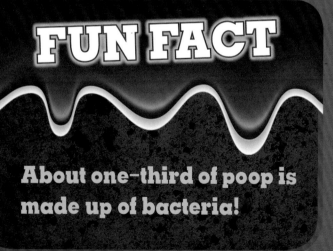

FUN FACT

About one-third of poop is made up of bacteria!

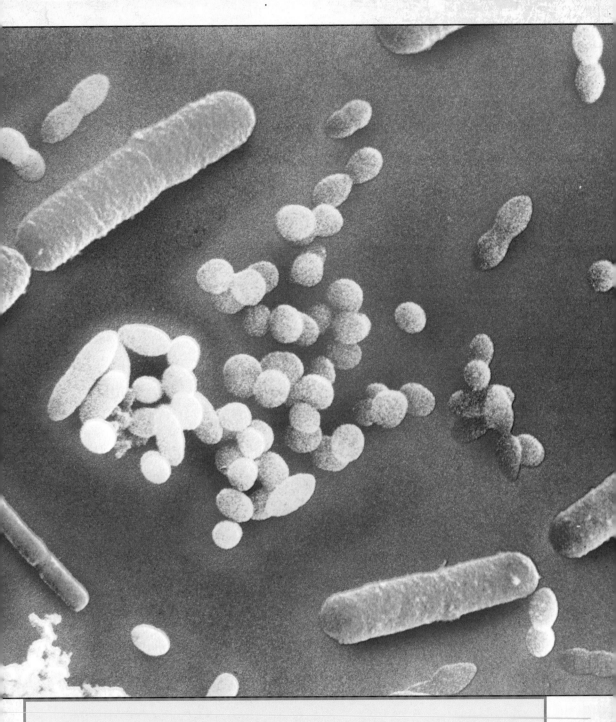

You may have as many bacteria cells in your gut as you have human cells in your body!

Ancient people knew about the power of poop. Today, some people still burn dry manure cakes to stay warm and cook their food.

guts, it picks up bacteria and scrapes off dead cells from our intestines.

Our bodies don't want poop anymore, but it's not entirely useless. People have burned animal poop for thousands of years as fuel for ovens and camp fires, and in some parts of the world they still do.

Plants capture energy from sunlight. Then we eat the plants, or the animals who ate the plants. Our poop still has some of that solar energy. Even fossil fuels got their power from ancient sunlight.

Squeezing Out Fuel

Once upon a time, an ancient amphibian paused to poop in a swamp. When it swam away, the poop stayed behind. Over time, the poop mixed with dead plants and animals. The whole mess was buried underground. Over millions of years, land and water pushed down and the spot heated up. All of this pressure and heat made coal, a fossil fuel.

Some researchers wanted to know what would happen when they squeezed and heated modern poop the same way. They created a setup that did just that. Fats in the waste helped the poop and toilet paper glide along the pipes of their machine. Out came fuel! They'd made a black, oily liquid called **biocrude**.

FUN FACT

US wastewater treatment plants could make 30 million barrels of oil a year!

To reach fossil fuels like coal, people dig through the dirt and rocks that cover them, sometimes hundreds of feet underground.

Biocrude doesn't look like poop anymore, but you still wouldn't want to touch it.

Biocrude can be processed into fuel for cars, trucks, and even jets. All this from a pile of waste many treatment plants pay to have taken away!

What's That Smell? It's Fuel!

When you flush a toilet, the contents speed along to the wastewater treatment plant. The treatment plants separate solids from the liquid. The solids go into bins called **digesters** that are closed away from the oxygen in air. There, the magic happens! The poop and everything that came with it changes through a process called **fermentation**.

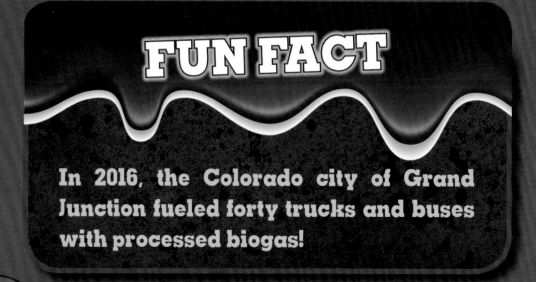

FUN FACT

In 2016, the Colorado city of Grand Junction fueled forty trucks and buses with processed biogas!

Digesters heat poop to keep bacteria happy; keeping the smells locked inside makes us happy!

This Swedish train is a gas! It's the first train ever to run completely on biogas.

Inside the bins, bacteria eat the poop and fart out something called biogas. Biogas is powerful. Some treatment plants burn the gas without using it to destroy it. What a waste! Others catch the gas to use as fuel. They still burn the gas, but they do so in a way that makes electricity. In this way, a treatment plant can help power itself.

Biogas can also power trucks, although first it must be processed. Biogas is a mix of methane, carbon dioxide, and other gases, including one that smells like rotten eggs. The fuel, methane, must be separated from the smelly stuff. Then it must be squished to fit inside a tank. Honk if you're powered by poop!

Running on Manure

Everyone poops, people and animals both! When livestock are kept indoors, their poop piles up. It still has energy and nutrients. Some farms put manure back on the soil to grow food crops. You probably don't want to think about that at lunchtime!

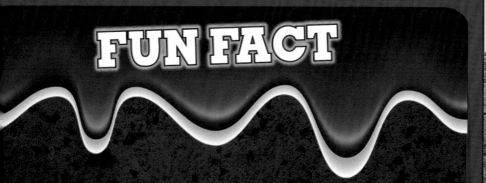

FUN FACT

A dairy cow that weighs 1,400 pounds (635 kg) can make about 112 pounds (51 kg) of manure in a day!

Don't throw that away! Manure makes power fuel that can be used on or off the farm.

Putting poop on soil is not always a good idea, and not because it's gross. Sometimes a farm has too much for its fields. Or, if the ground is frozen, poop might wash off into streams. Even though there is fish poop in the water, no one wants a pile of cow poop there.

When farmers can't use poop, they must store or dispose of it instead. It will rot anyway, so why not make fuel? Leftovers from fuel production can be used in crop fields. To use even more waste, some places mix manure with food scraps in the digester. Bacteria in the poop are happy to eat it all up, and when they poop, out comes the biogas! To use as fuel, the biogas can be piped away.

Two for the price of one. This factory uses milk to make cheese and manure to make electricity!

Poop-Powered Cars

FUN FACT

Hydrogen-powered cars can drive about 300 miles (483 kilometers) on a full tank!

Methane can be used by itself, or it can be broken down further to make a gas called **hydrogen**. Hydrogen is also a power fuel. Like biogas, hydrogen can burn, but hydrogen cars use a different method to get moving.

Gas takes up a lot of space, so the hydrogen gas must be squished to fit inside a **battery**. To make power, hydrogen and oxygen are brought together. They combine into water, and the process makes electricity. The electricity powers the car. Even though the hydrogen came from rotting poop, no one can tell. These poop-powered cars let out water as exhaust. Now that's refreshing!

This electric car charging station could use electricity powered by poop fuels. Smells better than regular cars!

Only special cars can run on this fuel. Hydrogen cars have been slow to hit the road because not many places have pumps for filling up with the gas. But by turning more poop into hydrogen, it could be available in more places. Poop is everywhere people want to be!

Number Two in Space

Imagine being an astronaut. Your ship is heading for the space station when suddenly you really have to use the bathroom—in low gravity. Watch out for flying bits! Luckily, modern space toilets suck everything in. But during a spacewalk, astronauts still have to wear diapers. There's no portable potty outside a spaceship.

Once astronauts use the toilet, there's the problem of what to do with the waste. Even when astronauts eat special diets to go to the bathroom less, poop piles up.

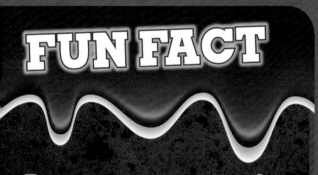

FUN FACT

Astronauts must practice using space toilets on the ground so they don't miss on a mission!

If you visited a space station, you would use a toilet like this one.

Astronauts have done strange things with it. There's poop buried on the moon! Some has been loaded into capsules and launched high above Earth. Luckily, it burns up in the atmosphere and does not become flaming waste hitting the ground.

The problem of poop in space will only get worse with longer missions. But people are working on bins that make biogas on a spaceship, turning a problem into an opportunity. Spaceships could fly on poop power!

FUN FACT

Poop-based fuels can help us use fewer fossil fuels. It also helps prevent envirnomental pollution.

The Space Poop Challenge received more than five thousand ideas to deal with waste during launches and space walks.

Journey to Mars

More rocket fuel would help a mission to the moon, but it would supercharge a trip to Mars! Can you imagine a colony on the red planet? People are working hard to make science fiction into reality. It's a race to see if the US government or a private company will get there first.

But whoever gets there first, it won't be easy. For one thing, it's a long trip. Mars is busy orbiting the sun on a different path than Earth is. Depending on how far away the two planets are at the time of launch, the trip could take seven to nine months. Considering that people poop about once a day, and that people definitely poop in space, that's a lot of time to make biogas!

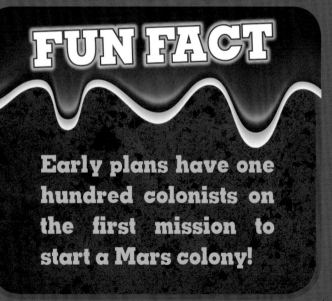

FUN FACT

Early plans have one hundred colonists on the first mission to start a Mars colony!

Falcon 9 was made by SpaceX, a private company that hopes to send humans to Mars.

Once astronauts arrive on the red planet, they will have to do everything by and for themselves. People will have to move machinery around, make new buildings, and complete other tasks that need

Any colony on Mars will need to protect colonists from the lack of oxygen and the dust.

power. Mars has lots of rocks but no gas stations or power lines. Colonists must use things they bring and things they make—like poop!

The Future of Poop Fuel

The next time you use the bathroom, think of all the things your poop might power. With all the great ways scientists have discovered to make poop fuel, we just need to make more of it! More treatment plants can stop burning off biogas and start catching it for power uses. More cars could run on hydrogen.

Nor are we limited by what we can do now. New ideas could find ways of turning poop into fuel that are easier, faster, and cheaper.

FUN FACT

Wastewater treatment plants could make as much as 12 percent of US electricity!

Poop could be an important source of energy for poor countries as well as rich ones. Where there's waste, there's power. Poop is available to everyone!

And poop fuel is pretty clean, despite the smell. It gives off fewer greenhouse gases than many fossil fuels. Most scientists agree that greenhouse gases in the atmosphere are changing the world's climate. Poop fuel could help save the planet!

Learn More

Books

Dickmann, Nancy. *Harnessing Biofuels* (The Future of Power). New York, NY: Rosen Publishing, 2017.

Mulder, Michelle. *Brilliant! Shining a Light on Sustainable Energy*. Custer, WA: Orca Book Publishers, 2013.

Sneideman, Joshua. *Renewable Energy: Discover the Fuel of the Future: With 20 Projects*. White River Junction, VT: Nomad Press, 2016.

Thisner, Martin. *Tag the Farting Power Plant: Silly Science Series #1*. Marin County, CA: CreateSpace, 2015.

Websites

Energy Kids, "Renewable Energy Sources"
www.eia.gov/kids/energy.cfm?page=renewable_home-basics
Explore the many kinds of renewable energy

Power Zone, "Power Sources"
www.enwin.com/kids/electricity/power_sources.cfm
The many ways we can get power

The USGS Water Science School, "Wastewater Treatment"
water.usgs.gov/edu/wuww.html
Learn why clean water is so important

Index

Published in 2018 by Enslow Publishing, LLC.
101 W. 23rd Street, Suite 240, New York, NY 10011

Library of Congress Cataloging-in-Publication Data

Names: MacCarald, Clara, 1979–author.
Title: Turning poop into power fuel / Clara MacCarald.
Description: New York : Enslow Publishing, 2018. | Series:
The power of poop | Includes bibliographical references and
index.
Identifiers: LCCN 2017022371| ISBN 9780766091023 (library
bound) | ISBN 9780766091009 (pbk.) | ISBN 9780766091016
(6 pack)
Subjects: LCSH: Waste products as fuel—Juvenile literature. |
Refuse as fuel—Juvenile literature.
Classification: LCC TP360 .M33 2018 | DDC 628.4/4—dc23
LC record available at https://lccn.loc.gov/2017022371

Printed in the United States of America

To Our Readers: We have done our best to make sure all
websites in this book were active and appropriate when we
went to press. However, the author and the publisher have
no control over and assume no liability for the material
available on those websites or on any websites they may link
to. Any comments or suggestions can be sent by email to
customerservice@enslow.com.